FIXED AND MOBILE SERVICES IN CERTAIN MOBILE SATELLITE SERVICE BANDS (US FEDERAL COMMUNICATIONS COMMISSION REGULATION) (FCC) (2018 EDITION)

Updated as of May 29, 2018

THE LAW LIBRARY

TABLE OF CONTENTS

Authority: 28

AGENCY

Federal Communications Commission.

ACTION

Final rule.

SUMMARY

In this document, the Commission amends its rules to make additional spectrum available for new investment in mobile broadband networks while also ensuring that the United States maintains robust mobile satellite service capabilities. First, this document adds co-primary Fixed and Mobile allocations to the Mobile Satellite Service (MSS) 2 GHz band, consistent with the International Table of Allocations, allowing more flexible use of the band, including for terrestrial broadband services, in the future. Second, to create greater predictability and regulatory parity with the bands licensed for terrestrial mobile broadband service, the document extends the Commission's existing secondary market spectrum manager spectrum leasing policies, procedures, and rules that currently apply to wireless terrestrial services to terrestrial services provided using the Ancillary Terrestrial Component (ATC) of an MSS system.

DATES

Effective June 30, 2011.

ADDRESSES

Federal Communications Commission, 445 12th Street, SW., Washington, DC

20554.

FOR FURTHER INFORMATION CONTACT

Kevin Holmes, Wireless Telecommunications Bureau at 202-418-2487 or
kevin.holmes@fcc.gov, or Nicholas Oros, Office of Engineering and Technology
at 202-418-0636 or nicholas.oros@fcc.gov.

SUPPLEMENTARY INFORMATION

This is a summary of the Commission's Report and Order, FCC 11-57, adopted on
April 5, 2011, and released on April 6, 2011, as corrected by an erratum issued on
April 15, 2011. The full text of this document is available for inspection and
copying during normal business hours in the FCC Reference Information Center,
Room CY-A257, 445 12th Street, SW., Washington, DC 20554. The complete
text may be purchased from the Commission's duplicating contractor, Best Copy
and Printing, Inc. (BCPI), Portals II, 445 12th Street, SW., Room CY-B402,
Washington, DC 20554, (202) 488-5300, facsimile (202) 488-5563, or via e-mail
at fcc@bcpiweb.com. The complete text is also available on the Commission's
Web site at http://wireless.fcc.gov/edocs_public/attachment/FCC-11-57A1doc.
This full text may also be downloaded at: http://wireless.fcc.gov/releases.html.
Alternative formats (computer diskette, large print, audio cassette, and Braille) are
available by contacting Brian Millin at (202) 418-7426, TTY (202) 418-7365, or
via e-mail to bmillin@fcc.gov.

Summary

The Federal Communications Commission makes additional spectrum available
for new investment in mobile broadband networks while also ensuring that the
United States maintains robust MSS capabilities. This action is consistent with
Recommendation 5.8.4 of the National Broadband Plan, which recommended that
90 megahertz of spectrum allocated to MSS could be made available for terrestrial
mobile broadband use, while preserving sufficient MSS capability to serve rural
areas, public safety, and other important national purposes. The rules adopted
herein: (1) Add co-primary Fixed and Mobile allocations to the MSS 2GHz band,
consistent with the International Table of Allocations, and (2) extend the

Commission's existing secondary market spectrum manager spectrum leasing policies, procedures, and rules that currently apply to wireless terrestrial services to services provided using the ATC of an MSS system.

I. Background

1. Mobile Satellite Service Spectrum Allocation. MSS is a radiocommunications service involving transmission between mobile earth stations and one or more space stations. As we discussed in the MSS NPRM, three MSS frequency bands are capable of supporting broadband service: The 2 GHz band ("S-band") from 2000-2020 MHz and 2180-2200 MHz, the Big LEO Band from 1610-1626.5 MHz and 2483.5-2500 MHz, and the L-band from 1525-1559 MHz and 1626.5-1660.5 MHz. 75 FR 49871 (August 16, 2010). Although the International Table of Allocations includes a primary Fixed and Mobile services allocation along with the primary Mobile-Satellite allocation in the S-band, such co-allocations do not exist in the U.S. Table. The Big LEO and L-bands are not allocated for Fixed and Mobile services either in the United States or on an international basis.

2. In addition, as noted in the MSS NOI, MSS has the capability to serve important needs, such as rural access and disaster recovery. 75 FR 49871 (August 16, 2010). MSS has the ability to provide communications to mobile user terminals anywhere in the United States, including in remote areas where people are without basic telecommunications services. MSS is particularly well suited for meeting the needs of the transportation, petroleum, and other vital industries. MSS operators have the ability to operate when existing terrestrial infrastructure is non-existent or has been degraded or destroyed and therefore can meet public safety and emergency communication needs in times of national crises and natural disasters. For example, MSS satellite networks were utilized in the aftermath of the terrorist attacks of September 11, 2001, and during the hurricane season of 2005. MSS units provide interoperable connections between emergency responders and other communications networks, and can even link U.S. emergency response providers with counterparts in neighboring countries.

3. Terrestrial Use of MSS Spectrum. At present, use of these MSS bands for terrestrial mobile service is permitted only under the Commission's ATC rules and in association with the existing satellite system authority. The Commission adopted the ATC rules in 2003. ATC consists of terrestrial base stations and mobile terminals that re-use frequencies assigned for MSS operations. In the MSS NPRM, we noted that technological developments involving the use of MSS/ATC spectrum could soon lead to the provision of mobile broadband services similar to those provided by terrestrial mobile providers. In particular, we observed that

SkyTerra (now LightSquared) plans to construct an integrated national satellite/terrestrial mobile broadband network, which would make use of both MSS spectrum and terrestrial spectrum that it has already leased in the secondary market, and that the services it would offer have the potential to expand services offered in the overall market of mobile terrestrial wireless services and to enhance competition in this larger mobile marketplace. In addition to LightSquared, three other MSS licensees have received ATC authority, although none of these currently has commercial terrestrial ATC stations in operation. We note that Globalstar's ATC authority has been suspended for failure to come into compliance with the ATC "gating criteria" as required pursuant to the temporary waiver granted in 2008.

4. Secondary Market Policies and MSS Spectrum. Currently, the Commission's secondary markets spectrum leasing framework, which applies to terrestrial Wireless Radio Services licenses, does not extend to ATC uses of MSS spectrum. In the Secondary Markets First Report and Order adopted in 2003, the Commission established policies and rules by which terrestrially-based Wireless Radio Service licensees could lease some or all of the spectrum usage rights associated with their licenses to third party spectrum lessees, which could then provide wireless services consistent with the underlying license authorization. 68 FR 66232 (November 25, 2003). The Commission provided for two different types of spectrum leasing arrangements for Wireless Radio Services: Spectrum manager leasing arrangements and de facto transfer leasing arrangements. Spectrum manager leasing arrangements require the licensee to maintain an active role in ensuring compliance with applicable Commission policies and rules but do not involve a transfer of de facto control under 47 U.S.C. 310(d), while de facto transfer leasing arrangements involve a transfer of de facto control and require Commission approval. In establishing these secondary market policies, the Commission sought to promote more efficient, innovative, and dynamic use of the spectrum, expand the scope of available wireless services and devices, enhance economic opportunities for accessing spectrum, promote competition among terrestrial wireless service providers, and eliminate regulatory uncertainty surrounding terrestrial spectrum leasing arrangements. At that time, however, the Commission decided not to extend these spectrum leasing policies and rules to satellite services. In particular, the Commission recognized that there already was a well-established set of policies and rules in effect for satellite-capacity transponder leasing, the kinds of leasing arrangements that were occurring in the context of satellite services. Satellite-capacity transponder leasing arrangements differ from spectrum leasing arrangements. Among other things, satellite-capacity transponder leasing does not involve the leasing of spectrum. Subsequently, the Commission extended the leasing framework to additional Wireless Radio Services and to Public Safety services, as well as to other terrestrial spectrum bands that became available.

5. More recently, as ATC services have begun to develop, the Commission has drawn guidance from the Wireless Radio Services secondary market leasing policies. In 2008, the Commission determined that its ATC policies specifically contemplated that MSS licensees could lease access to spectrum to third-party terrestrial providers so long as the requisite ATC gating requirements are met. Furthermore, the Commission found in one case that the particular ATC spectrum leasing arrangement at issue—which the parties had directly modeled on the requirements for spectrum manager leasing arrangements already available to terrestrial wireless services—was consistent with Commission policy, including the statutory requirement relating to transfers of control under 47 U.S.C. 310(d) that applied to Wireless Radio Services under the secondary market policies. Specifically, the Commission found that the leasing arrangement was consistent with a spectrum manager leasing arrangement under its spectrum leasing policies for Wireless Radio Services. Thus, even though the Commission did not adopt the terrestrial Wireless Radio Services spectrum leasing policies and rules for MSS/ATC spectrum leasing arrangements in a rulemaking context, it nonetheless applied the statutory interpretation relating to those policies and rules to the particular lease of MSS spectrum associated with an ATC authorization.

II. Discussion

A. Co-Primary Allocation of the MSS 2 GHz Band for Terrestrial and Fixed Services

6. As proposed in the MSS NPRM, we add Fixed and Mobile allocations to the 2000-2020 MHz and 2180-2200 MHz band. These allocations will be co-primary with the existing Mobile Satellite allocation. By adding these allocations to the band, we will be in a position to provide greater flexibility for use of this spectrum in the future. In addition, this change in allocation will bring our allocations for the band into harmony with the International Table of Allocations. We take no action on the proposal in the MSS NPRM that, in the event that a 2 GHz MSS license is returned or cancelled, the spectrum covered by the license should not be assigned to the remaining MSS licensee or made available to a new MSS licensee.

7. Our proposal to add Fixed and Mobile allocations to the 2 GHz MSS band received wide support from both satellite and terrestrial wireless licensees. Only Boeing opposed the proposal. Boeing argues that adding this allocation will undermine the ability of 2 GHz MSS licensees to provide service in rural areas, provide valuable service to public safety, and assist in disaster recovery. Boeing

also points out that keeping MSS primary in the 2 GHz MSS band promotes the goal of international harmonization with respect to satellite services. Boeing also claims that MSS networks provide the only means to create a next generation air traffic management (ATM) communication, navigation, and surveillance infrastructure. Boeing explains that it obtained a 2 GHz MSS license in 2001 with a goal of developing such a system but that economic conditions and other factors thwarted the plan. Boeing still believes that development of an ATM system is critical to the future of aviation.

8. We agree that MSS networks are a necessary and critical part of this nation's communications infrastructure, and serve an important role in meeting the needs of rural areas, the public safety community, and disaster recovery, but conclude that these needs can continue to be satisfied under the rules we adopt. MSS remains co-primary in the 2 GHz MSS band, which is consistent with international allocations. As we stated in the MSS NPRM, the addition of Fixed and Mobile allocations to the 2 GHz MSS band is merely a first step toward providing flexibility to allow greater use of the band for mobile broadband. The existing service rules that permit MSS and ATC operation in the band will not be altered solely by the addition of Fixed and Mobile allocations to the band. Both of the MSS licensees in the band will continue to operate under the terms of their existing licenses and must comply with all of the Commission's satellite and ATC rules. Furthermore, we are not altering the allocation for the Big LEO band or the L-band.

9. As to the development of an ATM system, we express no opinion as to the need for such a system, whether it should be satellite-based, or whether the 2 GHz band is a suitable location for it. As a practical matter, we note that Boeing has returned its 2 GHz MSS license. At the same time, there is evidence of exploding demand for spectrum for mobile broadband networks. Given all of the foregoing, we believe that adding Fixed and Mobile allocations to the 2 GHz MSS band will provide additional flexibility to meet this demand in the future and therefore is in the public interest.

10. We also modify three footnotes to the U.S. Table to be consistent with this change in allocation. Footnote US380 permits MSS operators to operate ATC in conjunction with MSS networks despite the fact that these bands have not been allocated for Fixed and Mobile uses. Because we have now added Fixed and Mobile allocations to the 2000-2020 MHz and 2180-2200 MHz band, US380 is no longer needed for this band. We amend footnote US380 to remove this band while keeping US380 in place for the MSS Big LEO and L-bands. Two footnotes, NG156 and NG168 permit certain Broadcast Auxiliary Service (BAS) and Fixed Service (FS) licensees, respectively, to continue to operate on a primary basis until December 9, 2013 (the sunset date for the band). Because the relocation of the BAS incumbents out of the 2000-2020 MHz band has been completed,

footnote NG156 which addresses the status of the BAS incumbents is no longer needed. Therefore, we remove footnote NG156 from the U.S. Allocation Table. We amend footnote NG168 to clarify that existing Fixed and Mobile operations in the 2180-2200 MHz band (i.e. the pre-existing FS licensees) shall become secondary after the band sunset date while ATC operations by MSS will continue to be permitted on a primary basis after the sunset date.

11. In sum, we find that adding co-primary Fixed and Mobile allocations along with the MSS allocation in the 2 GHz band serves the public interest. Our actions bring the allocations into harmony with the international allocations. We also lay the foundation for more flexible use of the band in the future, thereby promoting investment in the development of new services and additional innovative technologies. In adding these co-primary allocations and in applying certain secondary market spectrum leasing rules to ATC leasing arrangements we have not altered in any way the existing ATC service rules and policies that the Commission previously adopted to guard against harmful interference. Furthermore, we conclude that adding co-primary Fixed and Mobile allocations in this band will not result in harmful interference, and would not inevitably lead to uses that would result in harmful interference. Finally, having added co-primary Fixed and Mobile allocations to the 2 GHz band, we anticipate issuing a notice of proposed rulemaking on subjects raised in the MSS NOI, including possible service rule changes that could increase investment and utilization of the band in a manner that further serves the public interest. We expect the staff will take advantage of industry technical expertise as it develops options, which may include potential synergies with neighboring bands, to inform our decision making process going forward.

B. Applying Terrestrial Secondary Market Spectrum Leasing Policies to ATC Spectrum Leasing Arrangements

12. As proposed in the MSS NPRM, we extend the Commission's general secondary market spectrum leasing policies, procedures, and rules to ATC spectrum leasing arrangements. As we discussed in the MSS NPRM, recent and planned near-term developments in the use of MSS spectrum for the provision of terrestrial services are increasing the potential that these services will become sufficiently similar to the services offered in the overall market of mobile terrestrial wireless services to enhance competition in this larger mobile marketplace. Accordingly, we find that a common set of policies, procedures, and rules—where consistent with ATC policies and rules—will promote greater consistency, regulatory parity, predictability, and transparency with respect to spectrum leasing arrangements involving terrestrially-based mobile service offerings.

13. The record contains widespread support for this action. Indeed, every commenter that addressed the issue supported the extension of the general secondary markets spectrum leasing rules and policies to ATC. For example, the Telecommunications Industry Association asserts that applying the Commission's secondary market rules and policies to ATC will encourage innovative arrangements and partnerships that will speed the development and deployment of wireless broadband to rural and other areas. Additionally, Inmarsat states that spectrum leasing arrangements would facilitate the ability of MSS operators to deploy ATC, which would increase the availability of terrestrial broadband services and advance the public interest. Echostar notes that "efficient secondary markets * * * promote spectrum efficiency and create opportunities to maximize use of spectrum for mobile broadband services." We agree that applying these spectrum leasing policies and rules will help facilitate efficient and innovative new arrangements for using spectrum, including in both urban and rural areas. Moreover, commenters assert that by extending these spectrum leasing policies, the Commission would establish regulatory predictability and parity between similarly situated services.

14. Spectrum Manager Leasing Arrangements. Consistent with the Commission's ATC policies and rules, and the ancillary nature of ATC, we determine that MSS licensees and spectrum lessees may only enter into spectrum manager leasing arrangements. As discussed in the MSS NPRM, the Commission established several "gating criteria" that MSS operators must meet in order to be authorized to operate ATC stations. At their core, these gating criteria require the MSS licensee to provide substantial satellite service, as well as an integrated satellite/terrestrial service. We conclude that ATC spectrum manager leasing arrangements, which would require the MSS licensee to maintain an active role in ensuring compliance with all of these requirements, are the best means of ensuring that terrestrial leasing arrangements in MSS spectrum remains consistent with the underlying ATC policies and rules. We believe that the spectrum manager leasing rules will enable significant flexibility for the provision of terrestrial mobile broadband as part of an MSS/ATC service offering.

15. Under a spectrum manager leasing arrangement, the MSS licensee retains de facto control of the MSS spectrum at all times, remaining primarily responsible for ensuring compliance with the underlying ATC requirements (including the underlying authorization) as well as for the spectrum lessee's compliance with those requirements. This responsibility includes maintaining reasonable operational oversight over the leased spectrum so as to ensure that each lessee complies with all applicable technical and service rules, including frequency coordination requirements and resolution of interference-related matters. Permitting only spectrum manager leasing arrangements ensures that the MSS licensee retains primary responsibility for MSS, including the provision of

substantial satellite service (including all gating criteria) as well as the coordination of any terrestrial use with satellite use so that the terrestrial use is consistent with the MSS service and interference rules. Requiring spectrum manager leasing arrangements also address the concerns, expressed by Inmarsat, that the MSS licensee should retain ultimate control over the use of MSS spectrum in order to enhance its ability to coordinate operations and avoid harmful interference.

16. De facto transfer leasing arrangements, in contrast, would effectively transfer primary responsibilities for meeting these obligations to the spectrum lessee(s), which are not in a position to meet many of the underlying obligations of the MSS license, such as meeting the gating criteria obligations to provide substantial satellite service and to provide integrated mobile satellite/terrestrial service. Transferring de facto control over the use of the spectrum to a spectrum lessee also could sever the relationship between the provision of the satellite and the terrestrial service. We are not persuaded by the commenters that assert generally that we should permit MSS licensees to enter into de facto transfer leasing arrangements, but do not address how such arrangements would be fully consistent with the ATC gating criteria.

17. We also will apply the general policies and rules that pertain to the spectrum manager leasing arrangements, as set forth in the Commission's secondary market policies and rules. Accordingly, we agree with TerreStar that an MSS licensee may lease spectrum for ATC use in varying amounts and in any geographic area or at any site encompassed by the license when entering into a spectrum manager leasing arrangement.

18. Notification procedures. MSS licensees and potential spectrum lessees seeking to enter into spectrum manager leasing arrangements will be required to file the same information and certifications as required under the Commission's rules for Wireless Radio Service. As proposed in the MSS NPRM, we will require that leasing parties submit specified information and certifications (including information about the parties, the amount and geographic location of the spectrum involved, and other overlapping terrestrial-use spectrum holdings of the parties) to the Commission in advance of any operations that would be permitted pursuant to the proposed transaction. As is required with respect to a spectrum leasing arrangement involving Wireless Radio Services, each party to a proposed ATC spectrum manager leasing arrangement must have correct and up-to-date ownership information on file with the Commission (using FCC Form 602) as of the date that the notification of the spectrum manager leasing arrangement is filed.

19. As with spectrum manager leasing arrangements involving Wireless Radio Services, to the extent a proposed ATC spectrum manager leasing arrangement does not raise potential public interest concerns, the transaction would be subject

13

to immediate processing, whereas to the extent potential public interest concerns were raised (e.g., potential competitive harms, as discussed below, or foreign ownership concerns) the transaction would be subject to streamlined procedures as the Commission evaluated whether the public interest would be served by the proposed transaction. We hereby delegate to the Wireless Telecommunications Bureau (WTB) and the International Bureau (IB) the authority to resolve implementation and administrative issues relating to these notification requirements, which will include revisions to FCC Form 608 and the Commission's Universal Licensing System (ULS).

20. Potential competitive concerns. Assessing potential competitive effects of proposed secondary market transactions is an important element of the Commission's policies to promote competition and guard against the harmful effects of anticompetitive behavior. As the Commission recognized in the Secondary Markets First Report and Order, spectrum leasing arrangements potentially raise competitive concerns, and the Commission applied its general competition policies for terrestrially-based mobile services to these arrangements. Specifically, the Commission observed that it may consider the use of leased spectrum as a relevant factor when examining marketplace competition. In assessing the potential competitive effects of spectrum leasing arrangements, the Commission stated that it would determine, based on a case-by-case review of all relevant factors, whether services provided over both leased and licensed spectrum in specific product and geographic markets should be taken into account.

21. We conclude that spectrum leasing arrangements involving ATC also potentially raise competitive concerns, as several commenters assert. As we discussed above, technological advances will enable MSS licensees and their spectrum lessees to use ATC authority to provide mobile services similar to those provided by terrestrial mobile providers. While we recognize that in the past the Commission has not viewed MSS as a substitute for terrestrial mobile services, we have recently observed that the mobile satellite service industry currently is undergoing major technological advances and structural changes. In particular, we note that several MSS providers have, at various times, articulated their plans to offer high-speed data services, especially in connection with terrestrial networks using their ATC authority, and that such services in the future could affect, and potentially enhance, competition in the provision of terrestrial mobile services. Spectrum lessees using ATC therefore appear increasingly likely to provide services that could affect competition in the mobile telephony/broadband services product market. Accordingly, to the extent that we determine that particular ATC spectrum leasing arrangements can be used to provide such services, the procedures we will adopt allow us to assess these arrangements in the context of our existing competitive analysis framework for mobile telephony/broadband services, consistent with our general authority to ensure that the public interest

would be served by proposed transactions. We note that these procedures also enable us to assess each proposed spectrum manager leasing arrangement to determine whether any other type of competitive issue might arise in the context of the MSS/ATC transaction, such as leasing arrangements between different MSS operators.

22. Existing ATC spectrum leasing arrangements. We conclude that MSS licensees and ATC lessees must conform any existing spectrum leasing arrangement to the spectrum leasing policies adopted in this Report and Order. We note that providing this information and submitting the notification is consistent with the Commission's approach when it first evaluated an MSS/ATC spectrum leasing arrangement, as discussed above. We direct parties to submit notification to the Commission of any existing MSS/ATC spectrum leasing arrangements no later than thirty (30) days of the effective date of this Report and Order. This would include any spectrum leasing arrangement that parties may seek to enter prior to the effective date of the rules adopted herein.

23. U.S. GPS Industry Council's Request. In its comments, the U.S. GPS Industry Council expresses concern about the need to protect the Radionavigation-Satellite Service (RNSS) operating in the 1559-1610 MHz band, including the Global Positioning System (GPS), from interference from terrestrial operations in the MSS bands. The U.S. GPS Industry Council is concerned that applying existing secondary market rules to the use of MSS spectrum could lead to denser deployment of terrestrial services using MSS spectrum, which in turn would increase the probability of harmful interference to GPS. It also requests that the Commission codify the technical operating parameters applicable to MSS licensees under their respective ATC authorizations to ensure greater clarity and certainty about the interference rules applicable to secondary market arrangements. The U.S. GPS Industry Council expresses particular concern about potential interference to GPS that could result from adjacent terrestrial operations by an MSS L-band operator (LightSquared Subsidiary LLC). The National Telecommunications and Information Administration (NTIA) also has expressed concern about the potential for adverse impact of ATC operations in the L-band on GPS and other Global Navigation Satellite System (GNSS) receivers.

24. The addition of co-primary Fixed and Mobile allocations to the MSS 2 GHz band and the secondary market policies and rules that we adopt herein do not in any way change the obligations that attach to each MSS licensee to comply with the applicable technical and operational rules for ATC operations pursuant to its license. Under the spectrum manager leasing arrangements that we are permitting, the MSS licensee continues to have primary responsibility for ensuring compliance of any terrestrial operations with the obligations associated with its authorization, and each spectrum lessee would be obligated to ensure its operations comply with the particular technical and operational requirements

applicable to the MSS licensee from which it is leasing spectrum.

25. To the extent that potential interference concerns arise with respect to MSS/ATC operations in particular MSS bands, concerns will be addressed on a licensee and band-specific basis. We note that, as regards the interference concerns raised by the U.S. GPS Industry Council and NTIA about LightSquared's operations in the MSS L-band, LightSquared is working with the GPS community by establishing a technical working group to fully study the potential for harmful interference from its base station operations in the MSS L-band spectrum to GPS receivers in the adjacent 1559-1610 MHz band and to identify measures necessary to prevent harmful interference to GPS. Pursuant to the January 26, 2011 LightSquared Waiver Order, LightSquared cannot commence offering a commercial terrestrial service on its MSS L-band frequencies until the Commission, after consultation with NTIA, concludes that the harmful interference concerns have been resolved.

26. We emphasize that responsibility for protecting services rests not only on new entrants but also on incumbent users themselves, who must use receivers that reasonably discriminate against reception of signals outside their allocated spectrum. In the case of GPS, we note that extensive terrestrial operations have been anticipated in the L-band for at least 8 years. We are, of course, committed to preventing harmful interference to GPS and we will look closely at additional measures that may be required to achieve efficient use of the spectrum, including the possibility of establishing receiver standards relative to the ability to reject interference from signals outside their allocated spectrum.

27. Foreign Ownership. T-Mobile requests that, in applying the Commission's secondary markets spectrum leasing rules and policies to ATC, we extend the availability of the immediate processing/approval procedures to prospective lessees with indirect foreign ownership exceeding 25 percent, if that ownership has previously been approved by the Commission. We decline to revisit this issue here. T-Mobile's request is a reiteration of similar previous requests, including requests made in the Commission's earlier wireless secondary markets proceeding, which the Commission has denied. This Report and Order neither re-examines the wireless secondary market rules and policies generally nor establishes independent ATC secondary market rules and policies.

III. Procedural Matters

28. Paperwork Reduction Analysis: This document does not contain proposed information collection requirements subject to the Paperwork Reduction Act of

1995, Public Law 104-13. In addition, therefore, it does not contain any proposed information collection burden "for small business concerns with fewer than 25 employees," pursuant to the Small Business Paperwork Relief Act of 2002, Public Law 107-198, see 44 U.S.C. 3506(c)(4).

IV. Final Regulatory Flexibility Analysis

29. As required by the Regulatory Flexibility Act of 1980, as amended (RFA), an Initial Regulatory Flexibility Analysis (IRFA) was incorporated in the Fixed and Mobile Services in the Mobile Satellite Service Bands at 1525-1559 MHz and 1626.5-1660.5 MHz, 1610-1626.5 MHz and 2483.5-2500 MHz, and 2000-2020 MHz and 2180 MHz Notice of Proposed Rulemaking and Notice of Inquiry (Notice). 75 FR 49871 (August 16, 2010). The Commission sought written public comment on the proposals in the Notice, including comment on the IRFA. This present Final Regulatory Flexibility Analysis (FRFA) conforms to the RFA.

A. Need for, and Objectives of, the Report and Order

30. This Report and Order continues the Commission's efforts to enhance competition and speed the deployment of terrestrial mobile broadband. While ensuring the United States maintains robust mobile satellite service capabilities, in the Report and Order the Commission takes steps to make additional spectrum available for new investment in terrestrial mobile broadband networks.

31. The Report and Order takes two actions. First, we add co-primary Fixed and Mobile allocations to the Table of Frequency Allocations for the 2 GHz band, consistent with the International Table of Allocations. Under this allocation, Fixed and Mobile services will have equal status to MSS. This allocation modification is a precondition for more flexible licensing of terrestrial services within the band and lays the groundwork for providing additional flexibility in use of the 2 GHz spectrum in the future. The Report and Order does not change the status of the existing MSS licensees nor grant authority for terrestrial operations in the band beyond what is currently permitted under the ATC rules.

32. Second, the Report and Order applies the Commission's secondary markets policies and rules applicable to terrestrial wireless radio services to spectrum leasing arrangements involving the use of MSS bands for terrestrial services. Specifically, the Report and Order specifies requirements for licensees entering into spectrum manager leasing arrangements involving ATC, which will increase competition, improve spectrum efficiency, and allow small entities greater access

to spectrum.

B. Summary of Significant Issues Raised by Public Comments in Response to the IRFA

33. There were no comments filed that specifically addressed the rules and policies presented in the IRFA.

C. Description and Estimate of the Number of Small Entities to Which the Proposed Rules Will Apply

34. The RFA directs agencies to provide a description of, and, where feasible, an estimate of the number of small entities that may be affected by the rules and policies adopted herein. The RFA generally defines the term "small entity" as having the same meaning as the terms "small business," "small organization," and "small governmental jurisdiction." In addition, the term "small business" has the same meaning as the term "small business concern" under the Small Business Act. A "small business concern" is one which: (1) Is independently owned and operated; (2) is not dominant in its field of operation; and (3) satisfies any additional criteria established by the SBA.

35. Satellite Telecommunications and All Other Telecommunications. Two economic census categories address the satellite industry. The first category has a small business size standard of $15 million or less in average annual receipts, under SBA rules. The second has a size standard of $25 million or less in annual receipts.

36. The category of Satellite Telecommunications "comprises establishments primarily engaged in providing telecommunications services to other establishments in the telecommunications and broadcasting industries by forwarding and receiving communications signals via a system of satellites or reselling satellite telecommunications." Census Bureau data for 2007 show that 512 Satellite Telecommunications firms operated for that entire year. Of this total, 464 firms had annual receipts of under $10 million, and 18 firms had receipts of $10 million to $24,999,999. Consequently, the Commission estimates that the majority of Satellite Telecommunications firms are small entities that might be affected by our action.

37. The second category, i.e. "All Other Telecommunications" comprises "establishments primarily engaged in providing specialized telecommunications services, such as satellite tracking, communications telemetry, and radar station

operation. This industry also includes establishments primarily engaged in providing satellite terminal stations and associated facilities connected with one or more terrestrial systems and capable of transmitting telecommunications to, and receiving telecommunications from, satellite systems. Establishments providing Internet services or voice over Internet protocol (VoIP) services via client-supplied telecommunications connections are also included in this industry." For this category, Census Bureau data for 2007 show that there were a total of 2,383 firms that operated for the entire year. Of this total, 2,347 firms had annual receipts of under $25 million and 12 firms had annual receipts of $25 million to $49,999,999. Consequently, the Commission estimates that the majority of All Other Telecommunications firms are small entities that might be affected by our action.

38. Mobile Satellite Service Carriers. Neither the Commission nor the U.S. Small Business Administration has developed a small business size standard specifically for mobile satellite service licensees. The appropriate size standard is therefore the SBA standard for Satellite Telecommunications, which provides that such entities are small if they have $15 million or less in annual revenues. Currently, the Commission's records show that there are 31 entities authorized to provide voice and data MSS in the United States. The Commission does not have sufficient information to determine which, if any, of these parties are small entities. The Commission notes that small businesses are not likely to have the financial ability to become MSS system operators because of high implementation costs, including construction of satellite space stations and rocket launch, associated with satellite systems and services. Nonetheless, it might be possible that some are small entities affected by this Report and Order and therefore we include them in this section of the FRFA.

39. Wireless Telecommunications Carriers (except satellite). The Report and Order applies the Commission's secondary market policies and rules to terrestrial service in the MSS bands. We cannot predict who may in the future lease spectrum for terrestrial use in these bands. In general, any wireless telecommunications provider would be eligible to lease spectrum from the MSS licensees. Since 2007, the SBA has recognized wireless firms within this new, broad, economic census category. Prior to that time, such firms were within the now-superseded categories of Paging and Cellular and Other Wireless Telecommunications. Under the present and prior categories, the SBA has deemed a wireless business to be small if it has 1,500 or fewer employees. For this category, census data for 2007 show that there were 1,383 firms that operated for the entire year. Of this total, 1,368 firms had employment of 999 or fewer employees and 15 had employment of 1000 employees or more. Similarly, according to Commission data, 413 carriers reported that they were engaged in the provision of wireless telephony, including cellular service, Personal Communications Service (PCS), and Specialized Mobile Radio (SMR) Telephony

services. Of these, an estimated 261 have 1,500 or fewer employees and 152 have more than 1,500 employees. Consequently, the Commission estimates that approximately half or more of these firms can be considered small. Thus, using available data, we estimate that the majority of wireless firms can be considered small.

D. Description of Projected Reporting, Recordkeeping, and Other Compliance Requirements for Small Entities

40. This Report and Order applies the Commission's secondary markets policies and rules applicable to terrestrial wireless services to spectrum management leasing transactions involving the use of MSS bands for terrestrial wireless services. Leasing parties will be required to submit specified information and certifications (including information about the parties, the amount and geographic location of the spectrum involved, and other overlapping terrestrial-use spectrum holdings of the parties) to the Commission in advance of any operations that would be permitted pursuant to the proposed transaction. These changes affect small and large companies equally. To give these rules any meaning, this information must be generated by small and large entities alike. Otherwise, wireless service providers seeking to lease MSS/ATC spectrum would not have all of the information available to make educated leasing agreements.

E. Steps Taken To Minimize Significant Economic Impact on Small Entities, and Significant Alternatives Considered

41. The RFA requires an agency to describe any significant alternatives that it has considered in developing its approach, which may include the following four alternatives (among others): "(1) The establishment of differing compliance or reporting requirements or timetables that take into account the resources available to small entities; (2) the clarification, consolidation, or simplification of compliance and reporting requirements under the rule for such small entities; (3) the use of performance rather than design standards; and (4) an exemption from coverage of the rule, or any part thereof, for such small entities." 5 U.S.C. 603(c)(1)-(c)(4).

42. In the Report and Order, we add Fixed and Mobile allocations to the 2000-2020 MHz and 2180-2200 MHz bands. By adding these allocations to the band, we will be in a position to provide greater flexibility for use of this spectrum in the future, which may provide small entities with greater opportunity to lease spectrum. Only one party, Boeing, opposed the proposal, arguing the allocation will undermine the ability of 2 GHz MSS to provide service in rural areas,

provide valuable service to public safety, and assist in disaster recovery. Boeing also suggested that keeping MSS primary in the 2 GHz MSS band promotes the goal of international harmonization with respect to satellite services. Boeing also claimed that MSS networks provide the only means to create a next generation air traffic management (ATM) communication, navigation, and surveillance infrastructure. We agree with Boeing that MSS has an important role in meeting the needs or rural areas, the public safety community, and disaster recovery, but conclude that these needs can continue to be satisfied under the rules we adopt. Furthermore, we do not think it prudent to limit future flexible use of the 2 GHz band based on speculation that an ATM communication system may be developed in the band at some unspecified date, particularly in light of evidence of exploding demand for spectrum for mobile broadband networks. We believe that adding Fixed and Mobile allocations to the 2 GHz MSS band will provide additional flexibility to meet this demand in the future and therefore is in the public interest.

43. In the Report and Order, we take steps that may affect small entities that provide specific information pursuant to the Commission's secondary market leasing rules and policies. The requirements we adopt will require parties to an MSS/ATC spectrum leasing arrangement to file the same type of notification information that other parties to current spectrum leases must file. MSS licensees that propose to enter into MSS/ATC spectrum manager leasing arrangements must file the FCC Form 608. Additionally, all parties to such a proposed spectrum manager leasing arrangement must submit an FCC Form 602, which details ownership information, to the extent that a current version of this form is not already on file with the Commission. The extension of secondary markets rules and policies to MSS/ATC spectrum will promote competition in wireless terrestrial broadband and will benefit small entities in their efforts to compete against other wireless service providers, both large and small, in the provision of wireless broadband services. We believe that, on balance, the benefits to small entities of our actions in the Report and Order far outweigh any burdens this order places on small entities.

44. The record makes clear that broad support exists for extending the Commission's secondary markets rules and policies to MSS/ATC spectrum. Our actions in the Report and Order should benefit wireless broadband service providers seeking additional terrestrial spectrum, many of which may be small entities, by providing access to an increased amount of spectrum. Our actions benefit the public interest by promoting competition, innovation, and investment.

45. In extending the Commission's secondary markets rules and policies to MSS/ATC spectrum, we limit that extension to spectrum manager spectrum leasing arrangements. While several parties recommend we allow both spectrum manager and de facto transfer spectrum leasing arrangements, we reject those arguments. De facto transfer leasing arrangements would effectively transfer

21

primary responsibilities for meeting the obligations of the MSS licensee to the spectrum lessee(s), which are not in a position to meet many of the underlying obligations of the MSS license authorization, such as meeting the gating criteria obligations to provide substantial satellite service and to provide integrated mobile satellite/terrestrial service. Transferring de facto control over the use of the spectrum to a spectrum lessee also could sever the relationship between the provision of the satellite and terrestrial service. Thus, we do not extend de facto transfer spectrum leasing arrangements to the MSS/ATC spectrum.

V. Report to Congress

46. The Commission will send a copy of the Report and Order, including this FRFA, in a report to be sent to Congress pursuant to the Congressional Review Act. In addition, the Commission will send a copy of the Report and Order, including this FRFA, to the Chief Counsel for Advocacy of the SBA. A copy of the Report and Order and the FRFA (or summaries thereof) will also be published in the Federal Register.

VI. Ordering Clauses

47. Accordingly, it is ordered, that pursuant to sections 1, 4(i) and (j), 301, 303, and 310 of the Communications Act of 1934, as amended, 47 U.S.C. 151, 154(i), 154(j), 301, 303, and 310, this Report and Order is adopted.

48. It is further ordered, that pursuant to the authority contained in sections 1, 4(i) and (j), 301, 303, and 310 of the Communications Act of 1934, as amended, 47 U.S.C. 151, 154(i), 154(j), 301, 303, and 310, the Commission's rules are amended.

49. It is further ordered that the Commission's Consumer and Governmental Affairs Bureau, Reference Information Center, shall send a copy of this Report and Order, including the Final Regulatory Flexibility Analysis, to the Chief Counsel for Advocacy of the Small Business Administration.

50. It is further ordered that the Commission shall send a copy of this Report and Order in a report to be sent to Congress and the General Accounting Office pursuant to the Congressional Review Act, see 5 U.S.C. 801(a)(1)(A).

LIST OF SUBJECTS

Administrative practice and procedure, Communications common carriers, Radio, Reporting and recordkeeping requirements, Satellites, Telecommunications.

Communications equipment, Disaster assistance, Radio, Reporting and recordkeeping requirements, Telecommunications.

Marlene H. Dortch,
Secretary.
Federal Communications Commission.

For the reasons discussed in the preamble, the Federal Communications Commission amends 47 CFR parts 1, 2, and 25 as follows:

REGULATORY TEXT

PART 1 PRACTICE AND PROCEDURE

1. The authority citation for part 1 continues to read as follows:

Authority:

15 U.S.C. 79 et seq.; 47 U.S.C. 151, 154(i), 154(j), 155, 157, 225, 303(r), and 309.

2. Section 1.9001 is amended by revising paragraph (a) to read as follows:

§ 1.9001 Purpose and scope.

(a) The purpose of part 1, subpart X is to implement policies and rules pertaining to spectrum leasing arrangements between licensees in the services identified in this subpart and spectrum lessees. This subpart also implements policies for private commons arrangements. These policies and rules also implicate other Commission rule parts, including parts 1, 2, 20, 22, 24, 25, 26, 27, 80, 90, 95, and 101 of title 47, chapter I of the Code of Federal Regulations.

* * * * *

3. Section 1.9005 is amended by revising the introductory text and by adding paragraph (jj) to read as follows:

§ 1.9005 Included services.

The spectrum leasing policies and rules of this subpart apply to the following services, which include Wireless Radio Services in which commercial or private licensees hold exclusive use rights and the Ancillary Terrestrial Component (ATC) of a Mobile Satellite Service:

* * * * *

(jj) The ATC of a Mobile Satellite Service (part 25 of this chapter).

4. Section 1.9020 is amended by revising paragraphs (d)(2)(i) and (e)(2)(i)(A) to read as follows:

§ 1.9020 Spectrum manager leasing arrangements.

* * * * *

(d) * * *

(2) * * *

(i) The spectrum lessee must meet the same eligibility and qualification requirements that are applicable to the licensee under its license authorization, with the following exceptions. A spectrum lessee entering into a spectrum leasing arrangement involving a licensee in the Educational Broadband Service (see § 27.1201 of this chapter) is not required to comply with the eligibility requirements pertaining to such a licensee so long as the spectrum lessee meets the other eligibility and qualification requirements applicable to 47 CFR part 27 services (see § 27.12 of this chapter). A spectrum lessee entering into a spectrum leasing arrangement involving a licensee in the Public Safety Radio Services (see part 90, subpart B and § 90.311(a)(1)(i) of this chapter) is not required to comply with the eligibility requirements pertaining to such a licensee so long as the spectrum lessee is an entity providing communications in support of public safety operations (see § 90.523(b) of this chapter). A spectrum lessee entering into a spectrum leasing arrangement involving a licensee in the Mobile Satellite Service with ATC authority (see part 25) is not required to comply with the eligibility requirements pertaining to such a licensee so long as the spectrum lessee meets the other eligibility and qualification requirements of paragraphs (d)(2)(ii) and (d)(2)(iv) of this section.

* * * * *

(e) * * *

(2) * * *

(i) * * *

(A) The license does not involve spectrum that may be used to provide interconnected mobile voice and/or data services under the applicable service rules and that would, if the spectrum leasing arrangement were consummated, create a geographic overlap with spectrum in any licensed Wireless Radio Service (including the same service), or in the ATC of a Mobile Satellite Service, in which the proposed spectrum lessee already holds a direct or indirect interest of 10% or more (see § 1.2112), either as a licensee or a spectrum lessee, and that could be used by the spectrum lessee to provide interconnected mobile voice and/or data services;

* * * * *

5. Add § 1.9049 to read as follows:

§ 1.9049 Special Provisions relating to spectrum leasing arrangements involving the Ancillary Terrestrial Component of Mobile Satellite Services.

(a) A license issued under part 25 of the Commission's rules that provides authority for an ATC will be considered to provide "exclusive use rights" for purpose of this subpart of the rules.

(b) For the purpose of this subpart, a Mobile Satellite Service licensee with an ATC authorization may enter into a spectrum manager leasing arrangement with a spectrum lessee (see § 1.9020). Notwithstanding the provisions of §§ 1.9030 and 1.9035, a MSS licensee is not permitted to enter into a de facto transfer leasing arrangement with a spectrum lessee.

(c) For purposes of § 1.9020(d)(8), the Mobile Satellite Service licensee's obligation, if any, concerning the E911 requirements in § 20.18 of this chapter, will, with respect to an ATC, be specified in the licensing document for the ATC.

(d) The following provision shall apply, in lieu of § 1.9020(m), with respect to spectrum leasing of an ATC:

(1) Although the term of a spectrum manager leasing arrangement may not be longer than the term of the ATC license, a licensee and spectrum lessee that have entered into an arrangement, the term of which continues to the end of the current term of the license may, contingent on the Commission's grant of a modification or renewal of the license to extend the license term, extend the spectrum leasing arrangement into the new license term. The Commission must be notified of the extension of the spectrum leasing arrangement at the same time that the licensee submits the application seeking an extended license term. In the event the parties to the arrangement agree to extend it into the new license term, the spectrum lessee may continue to operate consistent with the terms and conditions of the expired license, without further action by the Commission, until such time as the Commission makes a final determination with respect to the extension or renewal of the license.

(2) Reserved.

PART 2 FREQUENCY ALLOCATIONS AND RADIO TREATY MATTERS GENERAL RULES AND REGULATIONS

6. The authority citation for part 2 continues to read as follows:

Authority:

47 U.S.C. 154, 302a, 303, and 336, unless otherwise noted.

7. Section 2.106, the Table of Frequency Allocations, is amended as follows:

a. Page 36 is revised.

b. In the list of United States (US) Footnotes, footnote US380 is revised.

c. In the list of non-Federal Government (NG) Footnotes, footnote NG156 is removed and footnote NG168 is revised.

The revisions read as follows:

§ 2.106 Table of Frequency Allocations.

* * * * *

* * * * *

United States (US) Footnotes

* * * * *

US380 In the bands 1525-1544 MHz, 1545-1559 MHz, 1610-1645.5 MHz, 1646.5-1660.5 MHz, and 2483.5-2500 MHz, a non-Federal licensee in the mobile-satellite service (MSS) may also operate an ancillary terrestrial component in conjunction with its MSS network, subject to the Commission's rules for ancillary terrestrial component and subject to all applicable conditions and provisions of its MSS authorization.

* * * * *

Non-Federal Government (NG) Footnotes

* * * * *

NG168 Except as permitted below, the use of the 2180-2200 MHz band is limited to the MSS and ancillary terrestrial component offered in conjunction with an MSS network, subject to the Commission's rules for ancillary terrestrial components and subject to all applicable conditions and provisions of an MSS authorization. In the 2180-2200 MHz band, where the receipt date of the initial application for facilities in the fixed and mobile services was prior to January 16, 1992, said facilities shall operate on a primary basis and all later-applied-for facilities shall operate on a secondary basis to the mobile-satellite service (MSS); and not later than December 9, 2013, all such facilities shall operate on a secondary basis.

* * * * *

PART 25 SATELLITE COMMUNICATIONS

8. The authority citation for part 25 continues to read as follows:

Authority:

47 U.S.C. 701-744. Interprets or applies sections 4, 301, 302, 303, 307, 309 and 332 of the Communications Act, as amended, 47 U.S.C. Sections 154, 301, 302, 303, 307, 309 and 332, unless otherwise noted.

9. Section 25.149 is amended by adding paragraph (g) to read as follows:

§ 25.149 Application requirements for ancillary terrestrial components in the mobile-satellite service networks operating in the 1.5./1.6 GHz, 1.6/2.4 GHz and 2 GHz mobile-satellite service.

* * * * *

(g) Spectrum leasing. Leasing of spectrum rights by MSS licensees or system